COSTA DEL SOL

MÁLAGA - MARBELLA - RONDA

TORREMOLINOS - BENALMÁDENA - MIJAS - EL BURGO
FUENGIROLA - CASTILLO DE SOHAIL - PUERTO BANÚS
ESTEPONA - CASARES - ANTEQUERA - VÉLEZ-MÁLAGA
ALGARROBO - TORROX - NERJA

BONECHI

INDEX

© Copyright 1994 by CASA EDITRICE BONECHI
Via Cairoli, 18b- 50131 Firenze- Italia
Tel. 55/576841 - Telex 571323 CEB - Fax 55/5000766

All rights reserved.
No part of this book may be reproduced without
the written permission of the Publisher.

Printed in Italy by
Centro Stampa Editoriale Bonechi.

Text by: *Giuliano Valdes*, Editing Studio-Pisa.

Translation by: *M. Rhiannon Lewis.*

Photographs from the archives of Casa Editrice Bonechi
taken by ANDREA PISTOLESI.

ISBN 88-8029-104-1

*Málaga, the Ayuntamiento (Guild-hall) :
photograph of the building showing
the Spanish coat of arms.*

INTRODUCTION

*W*hen one speaks to tourists and travellers about Málaga and its world famous Costa del Sol, an image of a stereotyped holiday resort immediately comes to mind. However the mention of Málaga also conjures up one of the most enchantingly beautiful holiday resorts which Spain can offer the hordes of faithful and enthusiastic tourists that visit its shores every year.

The city of Málaga is the capital town of the Province of Andalusia and looks out over a picturesque coastline, which lies between the Punta de Tarifa *(to the west) and the* Cabo de Gata *(to the east). Behind the sweeping expanses of the coastline, lie the mountainous reaches of the* Cordillera Penibética.

To the south of the town, the Guadalhorce *river - the largest river in the province of Andalusia - has, over the centuries, created the so-called* Hoya de Málaga, *which is, without doubt, the largest in a succession of small coastal plains which lie along this stretch of the shore.*

The highly singular features common to all coastal resorts are yet further enhanced by typically Mediterranean characteristics such as an exceptionally mild climate throughout the year (winter temperatures rarely drop to lower than 14°C while summer temperatures seldom go above 30°C), clear blue skies and bright abundant sunshine. All these factors serve to enhance the natural features of a landscape and an environment that is in itself both attractive and captivating.

The Costa del Sol is generally divided into two sections; the western part stretches from Málaga to Estepona; the eastern half stretches from Málaga to Nerja. Along this expanse of coastline (which has a decidedly Mediterranean atmosphere, thanks to the abundance of plants and trees which thrive here) a succession of beautiful riverside towns looks out over wide, long sea-fronts which are characterized by beautiful beaches of fine golden sands, gently sloping down towards the extraordinarily transparent waters of the Mediterranean Sea.

Málaga, a view of the Alcazaba (Fortress) and the Castle of Gibralfaro.

Málaga, a view of the Castle of Gibralfaro, the Guild-hall and the port.

MÁLAGA

The fifth most populated city in Spain, Málaga is situated along the flood plain formed, over the centuries, by the sediments of the Guadalhorce and Guadalmedina rivers. The city looks out over the azure waters of the Mediterranean Sea. Although it is on the whole a modern city, it still retains considerable traces of its glorious past and numerous important landmarks of great historical and artistic importance. The Guadalmedina river cuts the city in two: the more recently constructed districts are situated on the right side of the river, while the historical centre and the more ancient quarters are located on the opposite bank.

Together with its flourishing port and shipbuilding yards, Málaga draws its wealth from its iron, steel and metalwork industries. These are able to exploit the considerable amount of raw materials extracted by the area's thriving mining industry, which is located inland. An important contribution to the city's economy is also made by the food industry, while the surrounding vineyards produce high quality local wines (*sweet wine, "Maestro" wine, red wine,* *"Arrope" wine* -a concentrated grape syrup and *"Vino de color")* all made from the highly prized *Pedro Ximemes* grapes.

Founded by the Phoenicians, under Carthaginian domination *Malaca* gradually developed near the Greek colony of *Menace.* Conquered by the Romans in 205 B.C., it first became a *Civitas foederata* and then later, under the rule of Vespasian, became the *Municipium Flavium.* In the second half of the 1C A.D. with the proclamation of the *Lex Flavia municipalis Malacae* it was awarded the town charter.

After it had been conquered by the Visigoths and later by the Arabs, it became the capital of one of the kingdoms of Taifas.

In 1487 it was conquered by the "Catholic Kings" (the title earned by Ferdinand II and his wife, Queen Isabella of Castile); the rebellions of the Moriscos took place here in the 16C. Damaged by an English bombardment (1656), it was then captured by the French in 1810. The loyalist troops suffered defeat here during the time of the Civil War (1937). The city is also well-known as the birthplace of Pablo Picasso.

Málaga, the Fortress and the Castle of Gibralfaro.

Malaga, some views of the interior of the Fortress.

ALCAZABA

The Spanish word "Alcazaba" (or Alcázar) signifies "a fortified stronghold". The Alcazaba of Málaga, together with the Castillo de Gibralfaro (Castle of Gibralfaro) situated above it, make up one of the distinctive and characteristic features of the landscape of this Mediterranean city. Its robust ramparts, towers and bastions stand on a hillside covered by typical Mediterranean brushwood and shaded by pine trees, weeping willows and the elegant austere outline of cypress trees.

Further up, a curtain-wall connects this fortress to the imposing ramparts of the Castle of Gibralfaro which, from its elevated position, dominates the underlying city, the coastline, and the wide horizon, as well as the higher regions of the inland districts near Málaga. The first human settlements on the hill of Gibralfaro (which rises up to 130 m and literally means "the mountain of the lighthouse") seem to

have been established during the time of the Phoenician colonization of these areas. Some experts believe that the corner of one of the towers, which forms part of the defence system of the Alcazaba, could date back to the Phoenician period. Furthermore, remains of a burial ground dating from the same period have also been discovered. On this site, interesting funeral apparel and jewellery have been uncovered. However, it has been ascertained that the first nucleus of the Phoenician city was situated on high ground, on the site of the present day Alcazaba. The possibilities offered by this vantage-point were not lost on the new Roman conquerors who put its excellent strategic and defensive position to great use during their ambitious attempts to gain control over the "chess-board" of the Mediterranean basin.

According to the opinion of some experts, the present Alcazaba might even date back to Roman times. However , there is evidence to suggest that

Málaga, these photographs convey the grandeur of the Fortress and the stately elegance of its gardens.

the former structure was probably reinforced under the Roman insignia. Whatever the case, the landmark that can be admired by tourists today is certainly one of the most important examples of Arabian art and architecture in Málaga.

The present-day building, or at least its original layout, is the result of reconstruction work ordered by the King of Granada, Badis el Zirí, around the middle of the 11C. Unfortunately at that time, the entire Mediterranean basin was subjected to pirate raids. These inflicted not only great damage upon the coastal and riverside towns but also constituted a considerable risk for the inhabitants of these regions.

In fact, the construction of fortified strongholds and look-out posts was primarily undertaken in order to provide safety for the inhabitants. Even today, the numerous ruins of towers and fortresses dotted along the coasts of the Mediterranean countries, bear witness to one of the most turbulent periods of Medieval times, which have been defined by many as "the Dark Ages".

The considerable amount of work carried out by

Málaga, one of the gardens surrounding the Fortress.

Málaga, the famous "patio" (inner courtyard) of the Fortress

Following pages:
Málaga, an enchanting view of the "Patio" of the Fortress.

Málaga, architecture details and some Moorish features of one section of the Fortress.

Badis el Zirí on the Alcazaba resulted in the building taking on the appearance of a magnificent Levantine residence. In the 14C, the Arab sovereigns who ruled the nearby region of Granada (the splendid Alhambra provides admirable testimony of their presence there) transformed and enlarged the Alcazaba of Málaga.

After having conquered the city during the second half of the 15C, the Catholic Kings took up residence at the Alcazaba. Later, the splendid fortified residence was to become the home of King Philip IV (17C). During the 18C the building began to fall into decay and continued its relentless decline well into the 19C. The present-day building, which still retains its majestic and impressive appearance, was declared a national monument at the beginning of the 1930s. Later, painstaking restoration and reconstruction work was carried out in order to re-establish most of its original splendour. Particularly worthy of note are the elegant features of Moorish architecture which are to be seen in the building's courtyards (especially in the one containing a fountain) and in the porticoes, where slender columns support magnificent arches. These betray the characteristic features of Eastern architecture, being decorated with geometric designs and sculpted foliage motifs.

MOORISH ART

The origins of the term "Moorish" refer back to the region of Mauretania which, under Roman domination, comprised the present day countries of Algeria and Morocco. The Berbers settled in Africa during the period when the Islamic religion became widespread throughout the country, and this fact led the "Moors" to move towards the south of Spain (711). As a consequence, the Visigoths were forced to move northwards. During the period when the Moors controlled the region, a new style of art and architecture (later to become known as "Moorish") was developed throughout Southern Spain. Today,

These views of the Fortress of Málaga convey its stately elegance and the architectural versatility of Moorish art in Spain.

wonderful and important monuments and buildings still bear witness to this period of Moorish domination, which was later to spread northwards and down towards Africa. One of the distinctive expressions of Moorish art in Spain was the mudéjar style - a style created by the Muslim craftsmen who worked for the Christians. The origins of the Moorish style come from the Muslim tradition of the Umayyad Caliphs of Damascus and the Emirates of Cordova (7C - 8C). However the original style was later modified by the Almoràvids (11C) and the Almohads (12C). After the region was re-conquered by the Christians (1492), Moorish art and architecture became subject to decidedly eclectic influences, in which the mudéjar elements and features of Western art blend together to produce a pleasing effect.

Málaga, one of the rooms inside the Archaeological Museum and detail of a mosaic.

Málaga, Archaeological Museum: detail of a mosaic and a section created using the same technique.

ARCHAEOLOGICAL MUSEUM

The collections that make up this interesting section of the **Museum of Málaga** (another section is dedicated to the *Fine Arts*) are laid out in some of the rooms in the interior of the Alcazaba. However, a large number of exhibits which form part of the collections are not on show due to lack of space. The prehistoric collection consists of stone objects, tools made from flint, arrowheads, utensils and ceramics dating back to the Bronze age; there are also collections of funeral apparel which were discovered in the Phoenician tombs of Toscanos and Trayamar, as well as sculptures and busts dating from the Roman period (1C and 2C A.D.), mosaics transferred here from the Villa of Puerta Oscura and the lighthouse of Torrox, and a *Head of Epicurus*, a *Faun* and a statue of *Mercury*. The most outstanding exhibits dating back to the Islamic period are those which were contained in the Alcazaba itself, especially the ceramics and more particularly those dating back to the 10C and 14C. Pride of place goes to the ceramics decorated with a gilt finish - the result of a technique developed in Málaga between the 14C and 15C.

16

ROMAN AMPHITHEATRE

Numerous ruins of a Roman amphitheatre were discovered in a rather unusual and purely accidental way when construction work on the *Community Centre* was undertaken in 1951. It immediately became obvious that the tiers (which can still be seen today under the turreted buttresses on the western side of the Alcazaba) were an integral part of this important example of a Roman public building. It was probably built in the Augustan period even though references to the amphitheatre date back to at least the 3C. Its decline was accelerated by the fact that during the period of Arab domination, the architects of that time took building materials from this site to reconstruct the nearby Alcazaba. Some architectural features of the Roman period, such as the shafts and capitals of columns, have been discovered in the walls of the nearby fortress. Reconstruction work on the areas that once made up the proscenium is planned for the future.

Málaga, the ramparts of the Fortress dominate the tiers of the Roman Amphitheatre.

Málaga, the Community Centre and ruins of the Roman Amphitheatre.

*Málaga, a panoramic view of the guild-hall
and the Fortress.*

AYUNTAMIENTO (GUILD-HALL)

The setting of the majestic Guild-hall is beautifully enhanced by the surrounding gardens, palm trees and other plants that shade the wide avenues running along the sea front. This building, situated between the port and the lower reaches of the hill of Gibralfaro, was constructed between 1911 and 1919, after the town council offices (which had previously been located in the *Plaza de la Constitución*) were transferred to the edge of the *Paseo del Parque*. The latter is the result of large scale urban re-planning carried out at the turn of the century and based upon plans by the architect Manuel Rivera Valentín. The aim of the project was to lengthen the *Alameda Principal* by utilizing stretches of land which had previously formed part of the coastline.

This imposing and magnificent building has austere and elegant features - a factor which indicates that the construction is clearly an imitation of the

Classical style. However, it also contains features derived from Neo-Baroque architecture.

Plans drawn up for the actual construction of the building were completed by the architects Manuel Rivera Vera and Fernando Guerrero Strachan. The project also took into consideration the regional laws and stringent building regulations which had to be strictly adhered to during that time. The Guild-hall is a detached building and has corner buttresses which rise up like towers crowned with small graceful cupolas. The exterior facing is quite a remarkable sight and is decorated with pillars, numerous windows and columns. There is a vertical progression of prominent, elegant string-courses. The main entrance which looks out over the tree-lined Paseo del Parque, has rather ostentatious and yet decidedly elegant features which serve to heighten the over-all effect of its Neo-classical design. Particularly worthy of note are the large entrance surmounted by a semi-arch and the exquisite first floor portico, where the lateral double columns and those flanking the

Málaga, the main façade of the Guild-hall.

Málaga, these photographs show the grandeur and the elegant architectural features and sculptures of the entrance of the Guild-hall.

central section of the balcony create a graceful and harmonious effect. Upon the classically inspired tympanum (which gives this section of the façade the appearance of a Classical temple) is an extremely valuable sculpture depicting the *Allegorical Representation of the City of Málaga*. This work, together with numerous other sculptures depicting the *Kingdoms of Spain* which adorn the exterior of the building, is by Francisco Palma García. The sculptures which decorate the exterior of the side walls were done by García Carrera.

The stylistic features of its interior also contribute towards making the Guild-hall an extremely interesting building. A splendid and majestic flight of steps branches out into two lateral staircases. Particularly worthy of note are the sculptures of lions and vases which again are the work of García Carrera.

The effect created by the monumental grandeur of this flight of steps is further enhanced by the stained glass windows which are decorated with historical

scenes depicting *Málaga, founded by the Phoenicians, The Institution of the first Town Council, The Entrance of the Catholic Kings into Málaga, The Citizens' Revolt against the Admiralty* and *The Entrance of King Philip IV into Málaga.* Amongst the rooms contained within its interior, mention should be made of the *Chamber of Mirrors* and the *Council Chamber.* The former is decorated with paintings by Burgos, Oms, Murillo Carreras, Nogales and Vivó; the latter contains frescoes and paintings by Muñoz Degrain, Fernández Álvarez, Guerrero del Castillo, Capulino Jáuregui and Bermúdez Gil. Other rooms house the city's picture gallery. In fact, they contain works by artists from the 19C to the present day, including those by Revello de Toro and Ruiz Blasco, the father of the great Picasso.

Finally, the *Court Chamber* is also worth visiting as it contains a copy of the *Lex Flavia Malacitana,* the first known historical document proclaiming a city's autonomy.

Málaga, the eastern wing of the Guild-hall and detail of the architectural features and sculptures.

Málaga, two views of the majestic flight of steps of the Guild-hall.

Málaga, two view of the splendid gardens of Pedro Luis Alonso which frame the eastern wing of the Guild-hall.

Málaga, detail of the gardens of Puerta Oscura and Pedro Luis Alonso , the Guild-hall and the Fortress, and an aerial view of this scene.

THE GARDENS OF PEDRO LUIS ALONSO THE GARDENS OF PUERTA OSCURA

These gardens, which make up one of the numerous green parks in the city of Málaga, provide a decorative framework of trees and plants for the Guildhall. The **Gardens of Pedro Luis Alonso** are situated directly in front of the eastern wing and are laid out in such a way as to enhance the architectural features of the building, whether viewed from the Castle of Gibralfaro or from the top end of the gardens themselves. A fountain and a small round temple complete this idyllic location.

The **Gardens of Puerta Oscura** have a surface area of around 10,000 sq.metres and are particularly interesting as they contain a wide variety of trees and flowers as well as a large range of shrubs and bushes. The gardens extend as far as the hill on which the Alcazaba stands. The towering ramparts of the fortress stand out against the horizon and dominate the scene below.

Málaga, in the Paseo del Parque stands a beautiful 16C fountain known as the "Fountain of the Three Graces". The photograph shows some details of the fountain.

Málaga, views of the Fountain of Charles V (or the Genoese Fountain, 15C), situated in the picturesque setting of the Plaza de la Marina.

PASEO DEL PARQUE

The Paseo del Parque, which runs parallel with the *Paseo de España*, is a continuation of the *Alameda Principal*. This splendid tree-lined avenue runs from the *Plaza del General Torrijos* to the *Plaza de la Marina*. The so-called **Parque** is a small botanical garden and contains a wide variety of autochthonous plants as well as numerous species commonly found in subtropical regions. This entire area of the city is the result of an ambitious urban re-development scheme, in which land previously belonging to the coastline was utilized (1897) to create the so-called *nuevos muelles*.Amongst the most important artistic features of the area, note should be made of the charming **Fountain of the Three Graces** (16C), so-called because of the three marble figures upon it, and the **Fountain of Charles V,** also known as the *Genoese Fountain,* a beautiful example of Italian Renaissance design. The base of the fountain was added in the 17C.

Málaga, a view of the Castle of Gibralfaro and the Plaza de Toros (Bull-ring), known locally as "La Malagueta".

Málaga, a beautiful panoramic view of the Castle of Gibralfaro and an enchanting view of its robust castle-walls.

Following pages:
Málaga, a view of the ramparts of the Castle of Gibralfaro and a panoramic view looking out towards the Guild-hall and the Fortress.

Málaga, the Plaza de Toros (Bull-ring, 19C, seating capacity 14,000) as seen from the Castle of Gibralfaro, and an enchanting view of the city.

CASTILLO DE GIBRALFARO

The origins of this fortified stronghold, which dominates the city of Málaga from the top of a hill bearing the same name, go back to the mists of time. On this strategically important site there probably once stood an ancient prehistoric fortified village, perhaps a Phoenician defence structure: however, it has been ascertained that a lighthouse stood here during Roman times. The name of the castle is derived from the Arab words *Jabal-Faruk* which mean "the mountain of the lighthouse". More reliable sources refer back to a reconstructed fortress built during the time of Abderramán I (second half of the 8C); later, further modifications were carried out by Yusuf I (first half of the 14C). The castle, which today contains only a few remaining features of the original

Málaga, two views of the port district.

Málaga, some views of the port district and one of the splendid tree-lined avenues.

building (such as the encirclement of walls reinforced with barbicans, buttresses and towers), was once connected to the Alcazaba by means of an underground tunnel. Nowadays, only a curtain-wall connects these two fortified strongholds.

THE PORT

The large port of Málaga contains all the characteristics commonly found in any Mediterranean city which has always been associated with the shipping and fishing industries. This important infrastructure has always played a key role in the economy of the city itself and today it is still considered one of the principal maritime and commercial ports in the Mediterranean basin.
The port of Málaga is by far the largest in Andalusia and makes a significant contribution to the economy of the region, even if the fishing sector has suffered a certain decline over the last ten years. However, one should not overlook the fact that the port of Málaga still plays an important role as regards commercial and maritime trading with the nearby country of Morocco.

Málaga, the Cathedral (in the background) and the Fortress viewed from the Castle of Gibralfaro.

Málaga, the Cathedral and detail of the architectural features of the exterior.

THE CATHEDRAL

The splendid Cathedral of Málaga is one of the most remarkable monuments of the city. The construction contains various styles of architecture: this is due to the fact that the building took over three centuries to complete. As a result, the Cathedral has a Gothic configuration, a late-Baroque façade and yet the overall building is decidedly Renaissance in character. On the site of the present-day building, there once stood the Aljama Mosque which was later converted into a place of Christian worship with the advent of the Catholic Kings (1487). The construction was built in the Gothic style, but as early as in the first half of the 16C, it was decided to abandon the original project, and Diego de Siloé was entrusted with the task of continuing its construction. Work on the building finally came to an end in 1782. However its completion was far from over and even to this day it is known as *La Manquita* (a local expression which literally means a severed or missing limb). The suitability of this nickname becomes immediately obvious when one looks at the tower to the right of the façade. Although the tower has been built up to as far as the crowning part of the façade, its uppermost section remains incomplete.

The interesting **façade** rises up from a flight of steps

Málaga, the façade of the Cathedral, detail of the main portal and detail of the piazza in front of the Cathedral.

in the *Plaza del Obispo,* which is located in the centre of the city. Although it is comprised of two orders in the Classical style, it also has evident Baroque characteristics. The lower order has enormous portals which are inter-connected with decorative arches; the upper order has a colonnade running along it with mullioned windows with three lights in the lower section and single windows between the round windows in the upper section. The vertical progression of the façade, which is flanked by two towers, is decorated by double columns which are located on both the upper and lower orders. Above the main portal is a sculpture of the *Annunciation* by Antonio Ramos (1734); above the side portals stand sculptures of *St Cyriac* and *St Paula* (the patron saints of the city). Both of these works date from the 18C; the figure of *St Cyriac* was carved by Clemente Anes.

The **interior** of the Cathedral is majestically divided into a nave and two aisles by robust pillars and contains splendid vaults which have intricate carvings of decorative foliage motifs. The Cathedral also has beautiful stained glass windows, several of which depict historical and legendary scenes. Fifteen chapels open out along the aisles of the Cathedral and these (like the art works they contain) are largely Baroque in style. The most interesting are the **Chapel of Nuestra Señora de los Reyes** containing a sculpture of the *Madonna* (the former patron saint of the city) which was donated by the Catholic Kings (16C) and the **Chapel of S. Barbara**. Other interesting features in the interior include a 17C choir with 58 stalls, most of which were beautifully carved by Pedro de Mena, the two large 18C twin organs and the altar of the Incarnation, built of Carrara marble with agate columns.

Málaga, these photographs show the interior of the Cathedral, with details of the vaults, the pillars and stained glass windows.

Málaga, the interior of the Cathedral:
detail of the stained glass windows ,
detail of the ornate vaults
sustained by pillars.

Málaga, interior of the Cathedral:
a beautiful sculpture of "La Pietà",
detail of the high altar.

Málaga, nocturnal view of the Cathedral and a sculpture (Virgen de las Angustias) on the façade of the Bishops' Palace.

Málaga, detail of the beautiful façade of the Bishops' Palace.

PALACIO EPISCOPAL (BISHOPS' PALACE)

The Bishops' Palace, which boasts many fine architectural features, stands alongside the Cathedral, and when taken as a whole, these two buildings form one of the most interesting and important sights of the city. It was built in the 18C, its construction being supervised by the architect Antonio Ramos. Its splendid façade contains Late Baroque elements, even though many features common to Neo-classical architecture are also present. The three-storey building is crowned by an elegant balustrade, along which stand decorative elements resembling pyramids. The sequence of columns, the tympana above the windows and above all the elegant central section decorated with red marble columns and a niche containing a statue of the *Virgin of Woes* all contribute to confer elegance and grace to the building. By passing through an elaborately decorated wrought-iron gate one comes to the porticoed courtyard. The Palace houses the **Diocesan Museum of Sacred Art** which contains works by the young Picasso, Niño de Guevara, Valdés Leal, Jacinto Espinosa as well as copies by Correggio and Titian.

Málaga, a view of the Palacio (Palace) de la Aduana, detail of the Puerta de Atarazanas.

Málaga, the Puerta de Atarazanas, an example of Arab architecture in the city.

ADUANA (CUSTOM-HOUSE)

The present-day building was designed in the second half of the 18C by the architect Manuel Martín Rodríguez, although its interior was completely rebuilt after the fire of 1992. The building, characterized by the ashlar stonework of the ground floor, has graceful Neo-classical features. In 1810 it was occupied by French soldiers who inflicted serious damage to the interior. Later it was transformed into a tobacco factory before finally being turned into government offices.

PUERTA DE ATARAZANAS

This large gate which leads to the Central Market is rightly considered to be one of the outstanding examples of Islamic art in the city. Its present name dates back to the time when shipyards (*Atarazanas*) were once located in the vicinity. Its construction was undertaken during the period of Arab domination, during the reign of Abderramán III (13C). Worthy of note is the characteristic arch which displays the typical features of Arabian architecture and upon which can be seen the inscription *"God, alone, is the Victor"*.

Málaga, view of the Plaza de la Marina and detail of the entrance to the port district.

Málaga, fantastic water-games and lights light up the evening sky over Plaza de la Marina.

PLAZA DE LA MARINA

This elegant piazza in the centre of Málaga is situated between the *Alameda Principal* and the *Paseo del Parque* and constitutes one of the most characteristic spots of the city. Modern architectural features which manage to conserve the inherent characteristics of typical seaside districts confer elegance and grandeur to the numerous buildings which line the square. At the centre of the piazza a beautiful fountain spouting jets of water provides a lively feature to this throbbing heart of the city. Other characteristic features of this corner of Málaga are the palm trees, flower-beds and robust pillars which mark the entrance to the port district.

Recently, construction work undertaken to build an enormous, modern underground car park has greatly altered this characteristic corner of the city. The most significant alteration has been the removal of the statue of the *Cenachero* to the *Paseo de la Farola.*On the south-eastern side of the piazza, in front of the Alameda Principal, stands the **Monument to Don Manuel Domingo Larios y Larios.** The statue was carved by the sculptor Mariano Benlliure at the end of the 19C and the composition has obvious allegorical connotations.

Málaga, Plaza de la Merced: Obelisk to Generale Torrijos; Plaza de la Constitución: the fountain in the piazza and the Church of Santo Cristo de la Salud; Paseo de la Farola: Monument to "El Cenachero"

PLAZA DE LA MERCED
THE HOUSE OF PICASSO

In this piazza, which contains the **Obelisk to Generale Torrijos** (1842), stands the house of Pablo Ruiz Picasso (1881-1973). Up until recently, the house only had a modest plaque to commemorate the artist's birth. However, since 1988 it has been the seat of the *Picasso Foundation*.

IGLESIA DEL SANTO CRISTO DE LA SALUD

The church is situated near the *Plaza de la Constitución* which has a beautiful fountain. Dating back to the first half of the 17C, the church is a masterly example of Spanish Mannerism. The building is crowned by a cupola. The sculptor Pedro de Mena is buried here.

"EL CENACHERO"

The Monument to the Cenachero (the fish vendor) is situated in the *Paseo de la Farola*. This sculpture commemorates a local figure who used to sell fish to the housewives of the city. His basket of fish (*cenacho*) would either have been carried on his shoulders or tied to his elbows.

Málaga, picturesque view of the Pasaje de Chinitas; view of the Palacio (Palace) de los Condes de Buenavista which houses the Museum of Málaga (Museo de Bellas Artes).

This typical local character used to walk barefoot and wore extremely eccentric clothes.

PASAJE DE CHINITAS

This passageway,characterized by narrow stone-paved lanes and decorated with geometric motifs, represents one of the most picturesque corners of Málaga. The *tablao del Café de Chinitas* (which no longer exists) was once situated along the passageway and was a well-known meeting place for the *bailaores* and the *cantaores.* Here,García Lorca, found inspiration for the verses of one of his famous poems.

MUSEO DE BELLAS ARTES (MUSEO DE MÁLAGA)

The collections are housed in the turreted **Palacio de los Condes de Buenavista** (16C). Here, one can admire 13C-15C paintings of the Gothic school, Renaissance and Baroque paintings, sculptures by Pedro de Mena, works by Alonso Cano, Ribera, Benlliure, Gutiérrez Vega and paintings by artists of the Málaga school. Also to be seen are the famous *Anatomy of the heart* by E. Simonet and works by Madrazo, Sorolla and Moreno Villa. One room is dedicated entirely to the works of Pablo Picasso.

Torremolinos, an enchanting view of the coast.

Benalmádena, picturesque view of the
Andalusian village.

TORREMOLINOS

Torremolinos is the main seaside holiday resort on the Costa del Sol and is one of the most famous tourist spots of the Málaga district.
The first settlements in the area date back to the Neolithic period; later, it was inhabited by the Iberians, the Phoenicians, the Carthaginians, the Greeks and the Romans before finally being colonized by the Arabs. The origins of the place name are derived from the ancient Tower of Pimentel (14C) and some ancient windmills which today lie in ruins. In relatively more recent times (18C), a village was built on this spot, although Torremolinos did not expand into a large town until the 1960s. The large-scale urban development dates from this time and today the locality stretches out as far as Benalmádena Costa.
Amongst the numerous beaches of the locality are *La Carihuela* (which still conserves the typical features of a fishing village), *Playamar* and *El Bajondillo*.
A well-known sight in Torremolinos is the modern **Conference and Exhibition Hall,** designed in 1967 by Rafael La Hoz and Gerardo Olivares.

BENALMÁDENA

The localities which make up the extensive Commune of Benalmádena are situated in a pleasant scenic position along the lower reaches of Sierra de Mijas. As well as the picturesque village of Benalmádena, which is characterized by its typical white houses, the Commune is comprised of Benalmádena-Costa (which stretches out along the sea-front) and the village of Arroyo de la Miel. Originally a Phoenician and Roman settlement, it was expanded during the period of Arab domination and then taken over by the Catholic Kings in 1485. This small coastal resort has a large network of accommodation, tourist and entertainment facilities. The famous fun-park of **Tivoli World** is situated at Arroyo de la Miel; in the district of Benalmádena-Costa is the **Casinò of Torrequebrada**. The most well-known beaches include *Malapesquera*, *Santa Ana*, *Fuente de la Salud*, *Cajon* and *Torrebermeja*. Also situated in the locality is the interesting **Archaeological Museum**. Other interesting features in the locality include the ruins of a **Roman Arch**, a **Mosque** and the towers of **Bermeja** (13C), **Quebrada** and **Muelle** (16C).

Mijas, a photograph of the donkeys which are known locally as "Burros-Taxi" (lit. Donkey-Taxis).

Mijas, two enchanting views of the village and the characteristic Andalusian houses.

MIJAS

Mijas is a typical Andalusian hill-village which stretches out along the slopes of Sierra Mijas, the long mountainous chain which dominates the village below. It is surrounded by verdant dense pine-forests whose balmy perfumes permeate through the hillside air. The locality has become the favourite haunt of artists and foreign visitors who come here to enjoy this natural beauty spot, with its splendid green countryside, its breath-taking mountain scenery and enchanting views over the azure-blue waters of the Mediterranean and the snowy-white peaks of the Sierra Mijas.

The history of Mijas, like many other localities in this part of the Andalusian province, can be traced back to the eras of Phoenician and Roman colonization. Its rich subsoil - precious quantities of building marble were once mined in the district - constituted one of the many attractions of the area. During the period of Arab domination, the locality belonged, for a time, to the rebels of Omar-Ben-Hafsún (the ruins of the Castle which dominates the village date back to this period).

The urban lay-out of the locality is a noteworthy feature, particularly in the oldest part of the village: the picturesque white houses look out over the narrow lanes where local artisans sell their products to tourists and passers-by. Here, life can still be enjoyed at a leisurely pace and there is a marked absence of traffic and cars: in fact, the more lazy tourists and small children are given the unique opportunity of visiting the village on donkeys. These charming animals are known locally as *Burros-Taxi* (literally "Donkey-Taxis") and, decked out in their multicoloured harnesses, they make up one of the

Mijas, these photographs show the distinctive features of Andalusian villages: white houses, narrow streets and small piazzas.

Mijas, a view of the Sanctuary of la Virgen de la Peña and detail of its interior.

most characteristic features of the village.
In the district of Mijas, the beaches which are situated between Fuengirola and Marbella include, *Chaparral*, *Cala del Moral*, *Calahonda*, *Butibamba*, *Artola* and *Real de Zaragoza*.
Some 17C and 18C churches and chapels represent further interesting features of the locality -which also has an unusual rectangular-shaped **Plaza de Toros (Bull-ring)**. The most famous of these is the **Sanctuary of la Virgen de la Peña** which was carved out of the rock by the monks (1520). This atmospheric grotto, which is still visited by pilgrims and sightseers, contains the venerated effigy of the *Virgen de la Peña* (the patron saint of the locality).

El Burgo, features of a typical Andalusian hill-top village.

El Burgo, from the top of the hill, one can look down and admire the fertile agricultural land dotted with white Andalusian dwellings.

EL BURGO

This charming small village is situated in the inland regions of the Costa del Sol, along the *carretera* which connects the famous coastal resort of Marbella to the equally renowned town of Ronda. El Burgo is a typical Andalusian hill-top village stretching out on a rocky spur, situated along the north-eastern reaches of the so-called Serranía de Ronda. The village, like many other centres in this part of Spain, contains the characteristic features of Andalusian rural settlements, with its picturesque dazzling-white houses and small narrow lanes which seem to reaffirm the qualities of a more leisurely and relaxed way of life in a world where even tourism has now become a stressful, consumer activity. The rugged and fascinating countryside surrounding the village is dotted with crop fields and farms, which pay tribute to Man's hard work over the centuries.

Fuengirola, view of the coastal resort and the harbour.

Fuengirola, yachts moored in the tourist harbour and one of the local fishing boats.

FUENGIROLA

Fuengirola is an important seaside tourist town situated along the Costa del Sol between Torremolinos and Marbella and is sheltered by the towering mountains of Sierra de Mijas which loom up behind the town. Although the locality can boast an illustrious past, very few of its historical features remain standing. Nowadays, due to the presence of hotel complexes and luxury holiday apartments, tourists and sightseers visiting Fuengirola will come across a decidedly modern town. Having been conquered by the Phoenicians and the Carthaginians, the town went on to become a Roman colony. During this period in its history, it was known as *Suel* and elevated to the status of a *Municipium* (municipality). Under the Arabs, its importance grew considerably and it became known as *Sohail,-* the name being taken from a star which shone in the night sky towards the direction of the castle. In the second half of the 9C it was subjected to a Viking invasion; later, it was re-conquered by the soldiers of the Caliph Abderramán - a fact which

Fuengirola, one of the beaches and the Monument to the Pescador.

Fuengirola, view of the Paseo Marítimo and one of the ancient cannons which used to be situated in the Castle; a view of the Parish Church and the piazza in which the church stands.

was to lead to its partial destruction. At the turn of the 14C some Genoese merchants settled in the area which is known today as *Los Boliches,* and established thriving commercial dealings with nearby countries. Before being re-conquered by the Catholic Kings, the locality was destroyed in a fire, and consequently, was left abandoned for a long time. The place name Fuengirola would seem to be derived from *Font-Jirola,* a contracted form of the Roman expression meaning a stream, or it might even refer to the ships (*gironas*) used by the Genoese and Eastern fishermen.

The modern town can offer its visitors all kinds of entertainment facilities and it also has a well-equipped tourist harbour. Its beaches stretch for a total of 7 kilometres and include the enchanting *Playa de las Gaviotas, Playa de los Boliches, Playa de Santa Amalia,* and the *Playa de la Campana.* Features of particular interest to tourists include numerous *murales* (murals) which decorate some of its buildings (e.g. the so-called **Museo Abierto de Fuengirola** - the work of Spanish and foreign painters), the fishing district of Santa Fe de los Boliches and the ruins of a **Roman Temple** (reconstructed) along the *Paseo Marítimo.*

Fuengirola, the ramparts of the Castle of Sohail;
Puerto Banús, the tourist harbour, and the wharf.

CASTILLO DE SOHAIL

The Castle of Fuengirola stands in a scenic position on top of a hill close to the river Fuengirola and the seashore. In all probability, a prehistoric fortified village once stood on this site. Having been restored to its former glory after the Catholic Kings re-conquered Fuengirola (1485), King Charles I gave orders for cannons to be placed in the castle in order to defend the coastal settlements.

PUERTO BANÚS

The locality was built during the 1970s and is considered to be one of the most sophisticated and exclusive seaside resorts along the Costa del Sol. Yachts and leisure-craft owned by members of the international *jet set* are moored in the harbour; luxury hotels and apartment buildings as well as fabulous facilities combine to make Puerto Banús a marvellous tourist attraction. Those who love swimming and sunbathing can enjoy the splendid beaches of *Playa Puerto Banús* and *Playa Nueva Andalucía*.

Marbella, a view of the modern road that leads
to the famous coastal resort.

Marbella, a view of the tourist harbour and the
avenues along the seafront,
and a view of the beach.

MARBELLA

Marbella (lit. the *town of the beautiful sea*), as its etymology perhaps suggests a little too readily, stretches out like a shining jewel along the western part of the Costa del Sol, in front of a bay whose crystal clear waters have conferred a sense of timeless beauty upon this Mediterranean resort.

Even if this lovely Andalusian coastal town conjures up one of the most stereotyped images of a tourist resort, it should be pointed out that Marbella is a class above the other resorts in Spain and beyond. Situated between the open sea and the Sierra Blanca (which shelters the town from the cold air currents), Marbella has an excellent Mediterranean climate which not only fosters the growth of green and luxuriant flora but more importantly, encourages tourists and visitors to spend long holidays in this fabulous environment. First class accommodation facilities, three harbours for pleasure boats and yachts, an infinite variety of sports facilities (including a large number of excellent golf-courses) as well as the local bars, discotheques and the tasty local cuisine all contribute to make Marbella one of the best tourist resorts in modern Spain.

The urban lay-out of Marbella blends the typical characteristics of Andalusian towns (i.e. narrow streets lined with small white houses in the town centre) with the salient features of tourist facilities built here during the 1970s and the 1980s, such as the holiday villages, luxury hotels and apartment blocks. This mixture of architectural styles produces a pleasing effect upon the eye - a magical setting whose effect is heightened by the turquoise waters of the sea, its green gardens, an abundance of palm

Marbella, a view of the elegant Plaza de los Naranjos and detail of the fountain.

trees and the stern and yet protective outline of the Sierra Blanca.

The vast coastal front of Marbella stretches for about 28 kilometres, between Cabopino and Puerto Banús: the splendid beaches of fine golden sand which slope gently down to the sea include the *Playa de las Chapas,* the *Playa de Alicante,* the *Playa de Los Monteros,* the *Playa de El Pinillo,* the *Playa de La Bajadilla,* the *Playa de Venus,* and towards Puerto Banús, the *Playa de Casablanca,* the *Playa de Nagueles,* the *Playa de El Ancón* and the *Playa de Río Verde.*

The first settlements in the area date back to the Palaeolithic era, although the locality did not become a thriving town in its own right until the time of the Roman domination, after having previously been inhabited by the Phoenicians, the Carthaginians, the Greeks and seamen from all corners of the globe. Close to the site of the present day town, the Romans founded the centres of *Salduba* and *Silniana*; under Arab domination the locality became an important military and defensive stronghold. Later in 1485,

Marbella, majolica tiles decorated with religious figures; one of the typical streets and the bell-tower of the church; detail of the walls of the Arab Castle.

under the rule of the Catholic Kings, Marbella regained its status as a town.

The origins of its modern development can be traced back to the 18C and 19C when the town developed steadily as a result of the exploitation of considerable mineral resources mined at the nearby Sierra Blanca. In more recent times, the decline of its mining and iron and steel industries has been counter-balanced by a rapid growth in tourism and its related industries.

Among the features of particular interest to tourists is the **Villa de Río Verde,** an important example of Roman architecture which contains a beautiful mosaic floor, the ruins of the **town walls,** dating back to the time of the Arab domination and the ruins of the **Castle** (dating from the same period), which has round corner towers, walls and turreted towers. The simple elegance of the **Plaza de los Naranjos** which contains a beautiful fountain, is another noteworthy feature of the town. The piazza is lined with dazzling white buildings (including the 16C **Ayuntamiento (Guild-hall),** whose *Chapter-House*

Marbella, two characteristic views of the town centre,
where palm trees add a decorative note
to the Iglesia (Church) of San Pedro.

Marbella, two views of the excellent golf-courses.

contains a "mudéjar" ceiling) and has numerous or-
ange trees dotted around it. Near the Ayuntamiento
(Guild-hall) is a small well-laid out **Civic Museum**
(*Museo Municipal*) which contains exhibits dating
back to the Neolithic era, Roman artefacts found in
the centres and villas around the district and pieces
dating back to the Visigoth and Arab periods. The
museum also contains works by contemporary
artists. Also to be seen in the town are some 16C
buildings such as the **Casa del Corregidor**, the
Hospital of San Juan de Dios, the **Hospital Bazán**
and the 18C **Parish Church of the Incarnation**
(*Parroquia de la Encarnación*).
Finally, keen golfers should bear in mind that the
section of the coast situated between Nerja and
Sotogrande has 15 golf courses where they can
enjoy playing their favourite sport. These first class
facilities have earned the area the appropriate nickname of the "Costa del Golf".

Estepona, fishing nets laid out along the wharf.

Estepona, two views of the fishing port.

ESTEPONA

Estepona is the most westerly situated coastal resort along the Costa del Sol and stretches out in a beautifully scenic position along the foot of the Sierra Bermeja. It contains the typical characteristics of Andalusian small towns, even though its original urban lay-out also betrays evident Moorish features. Estepona is considered to be one of the most well-equipped seaside holiday resorts along the coast of Málaga and is also the most important fishing port in Andalusia

Modern hotels and luxury apartment blocks look out over the wide avenues along the sea front which are shaded by palm trees, while the town centre is surrounded on all sides by fertile rural countryside. Its magnificent beaches with their fine golden sands look out over the sea from which, in the west, the unmistakable outline of the Rock of Gibraltar rises up like an island from the marine depths. The numerous beaches of Estepona include the *Playa del Saladillo,* the *Playa del Castor,* the *Playa del Padrón,* the *Playa de la Cala* and the *Playa de la*

Estepona, a view of the beach, and two views of the beautiful avenues in this coastal resort.

Estepona, two views of the tourist harbour as seen from the avenues along the seafront.

Rada. The locality also has a nudist beach - the *Costa Natura.*

Originally a Phoenician centre (*Astapa*), Estepona became an important place during Roman times when it was known as *Silniana,* and had commercial dealings with the nearby *Salduba.* In the 4C, the Roman town was destroyed by a sea-quake. Later, it was re-built by the Arabs and given the name of *Estebbuna.* In the 15C, the soldiers of Henry IV of Castile captured the town for the Christians. Subsequently, the Castle of San Luis (16C) was erected in order to defend this part of the coastline from pirate raids and the present-day town gradually grew up around the fortress.

Interesting features of the town include the 16C **Castle of San Luis,** and a **Defence Tower** (dating from the same period); the 18C **Parish Church** dedicated to *Nuestra Señora de los Remedios* and the interesting **Plaza de Toros (Bull-ring)** which dates from the first years of the 20C.

CASARES

Tourists and sightseers visiting the inland district of Estepona cannot fail to be enchanted by the almost magical village of Casares, whose picturesque white houses are situated partly along a mountainous ridge and partly perched upon a steep rocky cliff. In this natural environment, characterized by mountainous territory which is in sharp contrast to the serene uniformity of the coastal region, one can gaze northwards as far as the peaks of the Serranía de Ronda.

Casares seems to be derived from the name of Julius Caesar (*Caesar*) who came here to bathe in its healing sulphurous waters. The locality is also famous for being the birthplace of Blas Infante, the greatest exponent of the Andalusian movement.

Casares is well worth visiting as it gives one the unique opportunity of admiring one of the most characteristic districts in the Andalusian hinterland. The arrangement of steep narrow lanes lined with white houses - a typical feature of hill-top villages - has unmistakable Arabian influences.

Casares, two enchanting views of this picturesque Andalusian village.

Ronda, a breathtaking view of the Tajo with the impressive structure of the Puente Nuevo (New Bridge).

RONDA

The mere mention of Ronda conjures up one of the most distinctive and certainly one of the most characteristic towns in Spain. It is situated at 750 metres above sea-level along a plateau surrounded by mountains (the Celtic name *Arunda* signified "surrounded by mountains").

The urban lay-out of Ronda is particularly interesting due to the typical character of its ancient town centre. Furthermore, one part of the town is situated at the edge of a steep rock-face, along the centre of which is situated a kind of canyon (the so-called *Tajo de Ronda*).

The Rio Guadalevín, a tributary of the Guadiaro river runs along the bottom of this deep gorge. One of the mountains surrounding the plateau is the Serranía de Ronda. The mountain road running across it connects the town to the Costa del Sol.

The district of Ronda was inhabited as far back as prehistoric times - a fact endorsed by the presence of the Megalithic monuments of *Los Arenosos* and *Cueva de la Pileta* (Palaeolithic graffiti drawn on rocks and Neolithic ceramics).

The origins of *Arunda* can be traced back to the Celtic Age; later, the Phoenicians settled in the nearby vicinity of *Acinipio*, which was formerly an ancient Iberian foundation.

After the Romans had conquered Spain, they changed the name of Arunda to *Munda* and turned Acinipio into a *Municipium* (Municipality), conferring upon it the inherent privileges associated with its new elevated status. In the first half of the 8C, the town was conquered by the Arabs who named it the "town of castles" (*Izn-Rand-Onda*).

After the Catholic Kings had re-conquered Spain

Ronda, detail of the Puente Nuevo and a view of the whole bridge.

(1485), Ronda enjoyed a period of great prosperity and extensive urban development which was to continue up until the end of the 18C.

One curious episode in the town's history took place towards the end of the 15C, when an association of eminent local citizens was set up to preside over the bull-races. This was known as the "Association of the Guilds" and many similar institutions of this kind were established throughout Spain.

The town is divided into two separate sections: the oldest district lies to the south of the Tajo da Ronda and is characterized by its medieval lay-out and unmistakable Arab features; this part of the town also contains its most important monuments and buildings.

On the opposite side of the Tajo lies the district of Mercadillo which was constructed during the 16C, although today it contains many modern buildings and most of the town's commercial activities and businesses are situated here. This part of the town also has some fine 18C buildings.

To the south, outside the town, lies the rural district of San Francisco.

PUENTE NUEVO (NEW BRIDGE)

Together with the *Puente de San Miguel* and the *Puente Viejo*, the Puente Nuevo connects the ancient town centre of Ronda with the modern district of Mercadillo. This bridge has became a symbol of the town itself and is a tribute to the architectural skill and audacity of its architects who constructed it between 1735 and 1793. The bridge, which is known as "Nuevo" (New), due to the fact that it was built to replace a former construction which fell into an abyss, is an extremely impressive sight. It has three spans, with a large central arch situated above another smaller one which has a much narrower bay. On the top of the bridge, two arches flank an enclosed area which used to be a prison, but which nowadays contains a shop. The bridge stands on robust stone pillars, is 98 metres high and is deeply embedded in the Tajo ravine, along which runs the Guadalevín river. This abyss, which has an overall depth of 180 metres, cuts the town in two, and is probably the result of a geological fault which split the rock on which the town stands into two separate sections.

Ronda, view of the Puerta Carlos V and the Alminar de San Sebastián; an enchanting view of the Iglesia del Espíritu Santo and the Iglesia de Nuestro Padre Jesús.

PUERTA CARLOS V

This beautiful Renaissance town-gate (16C) is set within the Arab town walls close to the **Porta de Almocábar** (13C). Nearby, once stood the Alcazaba, which was razed to the ground by the French (19C).

ALMINAR DE SAN SEBASTIÁN (THE TOWER OF ST SEBASTIAN)

What first appears to be a beautiful stone bell-tower, is, in actual fact, the ancient tower of a Mosque (*Alminar*). The building was later converted into a place of Christian worship and is built in the "mudéjar" style.

IGLESIA DEL ESPÍRITU SANTO

Situated close to the Arab town walls, the church was built during the reign of Queen Isabella of Castile in the 15C and was obviously inspired by the florid Gothic style.

IGLESIA DE NUESTRO PADRE JESÚS

This Gothic church has a beautiful stone bell-tower with Renaissance motifs. The interior contains beautiful Gothic vaults above the nave. Near the church stands a decorative 16C fountain.

Ronda, a view of the Iglesia de Santa María la Mayor, detail of the exterior portico.

Iglesia de Santa María la Mayor

Considered to be one of the most important churches in the town, Santa María La Mayor looks out over a lovely piazza dotted with palm trees and cypresses and is lined with the characteristic white Andalusian houses. The church only became a place of Catholic worship during the 15C when the Catholic Kings who ordered its conversion seem to have wanted to obliterate all traces of its Muslim origins. In fact, a 13C *Mezquita Mayor* (Greater Mosque) once stood on this site. Today all that remains of the former building is the lower section of the bell-tower, which has a Renaissance belfry on top of the *"Alminar"*(tower of the Mosque). The interior of the church contains beautiful 18C Baroque retables beautifully decorated with paintings and relievos.

PALACIO DEL MARQUÉS DE SALVATIERRA

This 18C building looks out over a small piazza containing a column with a cross on its capital. One of the outstanding features of the church is its elegant and refined Renaissance portal. On either side of this stand two Roman double-columns which support an architrave along which stands a balcony with wrought iron railings. The French window which opens out onto the balcony has beautifully decorated door-jambs on either side of which stand two pairs of Incan caryatides, believed to have been brought from Peru. On the top of the building is a triangular tympanum bearing a coat of arms with a crown.

Nearby stands the so-called **Casa del rey Moro**, a beautiful 18C building with an adjoining large garden.

Ronda, detail of the façade of the Palacio (Palace) of the Marqués de Salvatierra , detail of the ornate architecture and the Incan caryatides.

Ronda, detail of the sculptures in the Templete (small temple) de la Virgen de los Dolores.

VIRGEN DE LOS DOLORES

The construction known locally as the *Templete* (small temple) *de la Virgen de los Dolores*, is situated along the *Calle de Santa Cecilia*. This beautiful chapel is built in the Baroque Mannerist style. Particularly interesting are the motifs which decorate the pillars.

ROMAN BRIDGE

The name by which this construction is locally known (*Puente Romano* - Roman Bridge) is quite unsuitable when one bears in mind the fact that the bridge - a beautiful architectural construction - was

Ronda, two views of the Arch of Philip V (in the first photograph can be seen the "throne of the King of the Moors") which leads to the Puente Romano (Roman Bridge).

built in the 14C. It was completed during the period of Arab domination - a fact which becomes immediately obvious when one looks at the typical features of Muslim architecture which adorn the entrance arch. The arch is also known as the *Arch of Philip V* ; nearby stands a rather curious block of stone which is known locally as the *throne of the King of the Moors*. Other features of special interest to tourists include the **Plaza de Toros**. It is thought to be the oldest bull-ring in Spain (first half of the 18C).

It has a seating capacity of 5.000 and is the only entirely covered bull-ring in the country. One of the matadors who fought here was the famous Pedro Romero (born in the town in 1754), who is considered to be the "father" of modern bull-fighting.

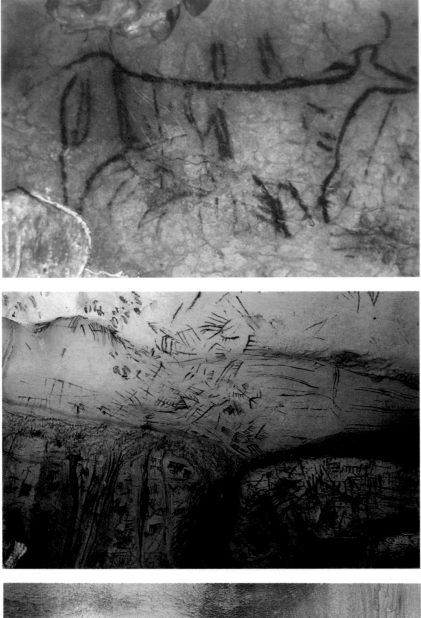

CUEVA DE LA PILETA

The cavern is situated in the part of the Serranía de Ronda which stretches out along the right banks of the Guadiaro river. Due to its great speleological interest, its wealth of concretions, and above all to the excellent prehistoric features it contains, it was declared a national monument in 1924. It was discovered during the first years of the 20C, but only became famous after it was explored by an English officer. The entrance to the cave is situated at 700 metres above sea-level and it leads into a fascinating underground kingdom of caves, stalactites and stalagmites. Numerous ceramics and utensils dating back to the Palaeolithic and Neolithic eras have been found deep within the cave. Some black, ochre, yellow and red graffiti scribbled on the rock walls, constitute another interesting feature inside the cavern. Experts believe that these date back to over 240 centuries ago.

Cueva de la Pileta, photographs of the Neolithic graffiti scribbled on the rock walls of the cave.

PARQUE NATURAL DE "EL TORCAL"

This vast protected area, set in a beautiful natural landscape, stretches out over most of the Sierra del Torcal, which lies a little to the south of Antequera, on the road towards Málaga.

The Nature Park was set up in 1978 in order to protect an extremely interesting naturalist area.

It is well worth visiting this bizarre natural phenomenon, although tourists and ramblers are advised not to stray off the well-signposted routes.

The wind and other atmospheric conditions have eroded the Karst rocks, producing some bizarre and unusual rock formations, and give the visitor the impression of being in a petrified town.

Looking out over this fantastic scene gives one the impression of being in a magical world, where the wind blowing through the rocks creates an eerie atmosphere.

El Torcal, some views of the extraordinary rock shapes formed by erosion on the Sierra del Torcal.

Antequera, a panoramic view.

Antequera, the Arco de los Gigantes is set within the ancient castle walls.

Antequera, a view of the beautiful plateresque façade of the Real Colegiata de Santa María la Mayor.

ANTEQUERA

This important city in the inland district of Málaga is situated along the bottom of the Sierra del Torcal, at the basin of the Guadalhorce river. The plain of Antequera - which is, in actual fact, situated on a hill at 500 metres above sea-level,- is surrounded by the mountains of Las Cabras, Los Torcales, Abdalajís, Chimeneas, Arcas and Camorra.

Antequera is a typical Andalusian town of great urban and architectural interest and has some interesting landmarks and buildings. Megalithic monuments found in the surrounding district are considered to be amongst the most important ones discovered in the Old Continent (Asia and Europe). These include the **dolmens of Menga, Viera** and **Romeral**, which dates back to over 45 centuries ago.

The origins of the present town can be traced back to the time of the Roman domination, when it was named *Anticuaria* and elevated to the status of a *Municipium* (Municipality).

Under Muslim domination, it was known as *Antakira* and equipped with an impregnable defence structure which enabled the city to defend itself from numerous sieges. The prince regent, Don Fernando, led the troops which re-conquered the city for the Catholic cause in 1410. However, the city's period of greatest prosperity occurred during the 17C and 18C, when, in particular, painting, sculpture and architecture flourished greatly. The urban lay-out of the city is characterized by typical Andalusian features (e.g. dazzling white houses), but it also contains many beautiful Renaissance and Baroque constructions which make Antequera one of the most interesting tourist attractions around the inland district of Málaga. One of its most interesting features includes the **Cathedral,** also known as the *Real Colegiata de Santa María la Mayor,* built in the first half of the 16C. Its beautiful plateresque façade is decorated with large arches and geometrical motifs.

The uppermost section has three triangular tympana and numerous pinnacles. The Renaissance interior,

Antequera, these views show the unusual Portichuelo, the Palacio (Palace) de Nájera (which houses the City Museum), and a detail of the Arab castle.

with one nave and two aisles, contains "mudéjar" decorations. Nearby stands the **Arco (Arch) de los Gigantes** (16C). Also worth visiting is the unusual building known as the **Portichuelo** (18C) and the ruins of the **Alcazaba** (an ancient Arab fortress). The latter, built on top of Roman ruins, has a square tower called *La Blanca* (13C). Another tower added during the Renaissance period, is known as *Del Homenaje*. The **Palace of Nájera**(17C) contains the **Museo Municipal** (City Museum), which amongst the many exhibits on show, contains the famous *Ephebus of Antequera*, a Roman sculpture in bronze, which dates back to the 1C A.D.

Cueva de Menga, some views of the Megalithic chamber tombs: the entrance, the burial chamber and the antechamber (vestibule).

CUEVA DE MENGA

A little outside the town, on the road leading towards Granada, are some extremely interesting Megalithic monuments which are known as the *Cueva del Romeral,* the *Cueva de Menga* and the *Cueva de Viera.* These are dolmens (large Megalithic chamber tombs) which date back to at least twenty five centuries before the birth of Christ. The largest and oldest of the three is the Cueva de Menga. The burial chamber with its central monolithic pillars, the antechamber (or vestibule) and the entrance of the tomb, are all features which are reminiscent of Etruscan burial tombs.

Vélez-Málaga, an enchanting view of the town dominated by the Arab castle and a beautiful view towards the bell-tower of the Iglesia de Santa María.

VÉLEZ-MÁLAGA

Vélez-Málaga is a beautiful small town which contains many interesting features. It is situated a short distance from the coast, huddled around a hill lying to the left of the river Vélez. Formerly an ancient Phoenician, Carthaginian and Roman settlement (some experts even believe that the Greek colony of *Mainake* was also situated along the coast), Vélez grew in importance during the time of the Arab domination. Later it was reconquered by Ferdinand II (the "Catholic King"). The turreted Arab **Castle** (13C) dominates the town. The beautiful Gothic-mudejar **Church of Santa María la Mayor** (16C), with a basilican lay-out (double colonnade and apse), a nave and two aisles, and a beautiful 16C retable decorated with paintings and relievos at the high altar and the **Church of San Juan Bautista (St John the Baptist)** (16C, built on the site of a pre-existing Mosque, containing a marvellous *Crucifixion* in polychrome wood, attributed to 16C Castilian artists) are just two of the interesting churches situated in the town.

ALGARROBO

Algarrobo is a picturesque village characterized by typical Andalusian features. The coastal district contains modern luxury apartments. In this charming locality, the houses seem to have been built one on top of the other, and their colourful façades are in sharp contrast to the hills lying behind the village.

Nearby stands a Phoenician burial-ground, known as the **Necropolis of Trayamar**. The **Hermitage of St Sebastian**, surrounded by palm trees and gardens is also situated close to the village. This building betrays the characteristic architectural features of Spanish places of worship: the simple, elegant white façade is vertically divided by two pilaster-strips and a beautiful bell-tower dominates the building from above. The small coastal village of Algarrobo-Costa has modern, well-equipped accommodation facilities.

Algarrobo, a picturesque view of this enchanting Andalusian village and a view of the Hermitage of St Sebastian, surrounded by gardens.

TORROX

The town of Torrox is divided into two separate districts: the bathing facilities and seaside resort are situated along the Costa del Sol, while the more ancient and prevalently rural district is set out along a mountainous slope.

A Roman necropolis has been discovered in the area, and this, together with other archaeological finds, prove the existence of the ancient *Caviculum*. This was originally a Roman staging-post, although it soon developed into quite an important town. The Romans were particularly attracted by the pleasant features of these areas and stayed here from the 1C A.D. to the 4C. The numerous finds made in the district include some ceramics, the ruins of spa-buildings and a vessel which was used to prepare *garum* - a kind of sauce eaten as an accompaniment to fish.

Along the coast, which is dominated by two defence **Towers,** lie the beautiful beaches of *Playas de Ferrara, El Morche, Peñoncillo* and *Calaceite*.

Torrox, an enchanting view of the hillside village and a view of the wide beach situated along the coastal district of the town.

Nerja, a view of the enchanting beach of Calahonda and a view of the "Balcony of Europe".

NERJA

Situated in a pleasant geographical position, Nerja is the easternmost locality of the Costa del Sol. It is a well-known seaside and residential resort, stretching out along a rocky ledge facing the sea and is sheltered by the mountains of the Sierra de Almijara.

The first settlements in the district of present-day Nerja date back to prehistoric times - as the graffiti discovered in a nearby cave have proved. In ancient times, due to its pleasant setting, the town was a popular stopping-off point with sailors exploring this stretch of the Andalusian coastline. In the vicinity, the Romans founded a settlement known as *Detunda*, although the town enjoyed its period of greatest prosperity during the period of Arab domination (when it was known as *Narixa* or *Narija*, meaning "an abundant stream").

Interesting buildings in the town include the **Church of El Salvador** (17C-18C) and the 18C **Hermitage of la Señora de las Angustias**, also known as the *Chapel of Mercy*. The marvellous **look-out post** situated on the top of the ancient fortress is known as the *Balcony of Europe*.

Cueva de Nerja, these photographs show some of the interesting features of the cavern, in which Neolithic graffiti scribbled on rock walls have been discovered.

CUEVA DE NERJA

This cavern is one of the most interesting tourist attractions along the Costa del Sol and is situated a short distance outside the coastal resort of Nerja. It was discovered almost by chance at the end of the 1950s and declared a national monument. Inside the cavern, a large number of Karst phenomena have resulted in the formation of caves, stalactites and stalagmites - creating a unique and atmospheric environment.

Experts believe that the cavern dates back to prehistoric times; in fact, the black, red and yellow graffiti scribbled on the rocks date back to the Neolithic era. Amongst the numerous caves which make up this underground kingdom are the *Sala* (Cave) *de la Cascada,* the *Sala del Cataclismo,* and the *Sala de los Fantasmas.* Concerts and ballet performances are put on here during the summer months. Another part of the cavern has been transformed into an **Archaeological Museum** which contains exhibits found in the grotto.

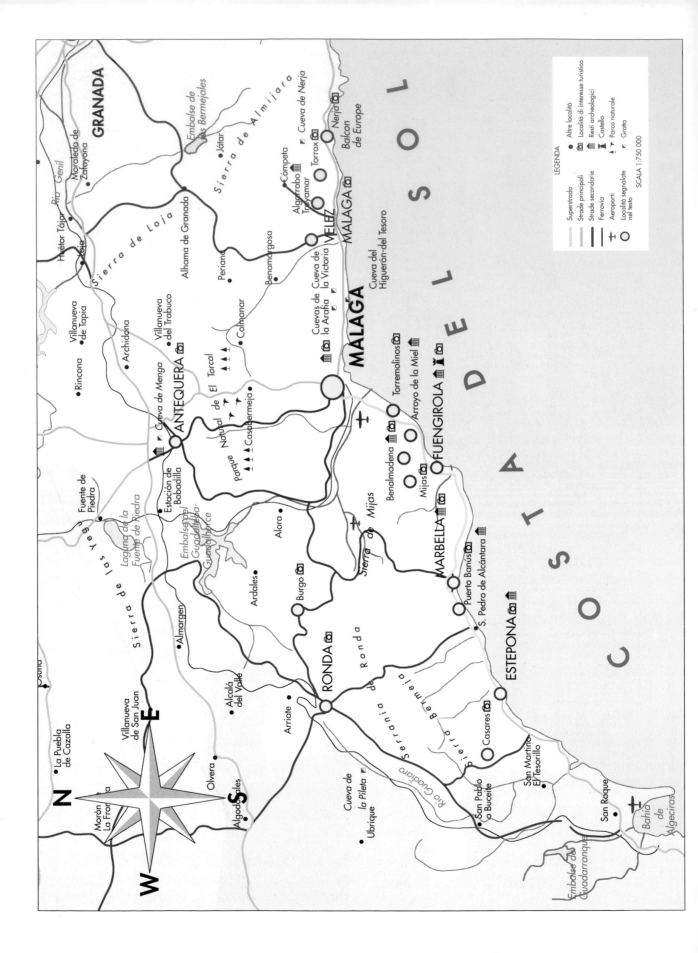